Better Homes and Gardens

Sewing
Casual Clothes

MEREDITH PRESS

NEW YORK   DES MOINES

BETTER HOMES AND GARDENS CREATIVE SEWING LIBRARY, FIRST PRINTING

©MEREDITH PUBLISHING COMPANY, 1966. ALL RIGHTS RESERVED

PRINTED IN THE UNITED STATES OF AMERICA

CREATIVE SEWING

Beautiful fabrics and exciting pattern styles make sewing more rewarding than ever. With today's new techniques and equipment, sewing can be fun for the beginner as well as the accomplished seamstress.

Better Homes and Gardens Creative Sewing Library presents sewing methods based on common sense— practical, professional tips that show how to give clothes for the whole family a "custom-made" look.

The Creative Sewing Library has been prepared under the guidance of Miss Lucille Rivers, one of America's eminent sewing experts. To help women learn the easy, professional methods of sewing she describes in the books, she has drawn upon her long experience in the field. Miss Rivers has directed her own custom salon in New York, and she has served as consultant to many leading clothing manufacturers.

She has created new styles for fashion shows, and has lectured on sewing in department stores in this country, Australia, and New Zealand. For many years Miss Rivers was sewing editor of NBC's popular "Home Show," and she has conducted sewing demonstrations on many other television programs. In the Creative Sewing Library, she shares her fashion knowledge and dressmaking experience with you.

Titles in the Creative Sewing Library are:
> *Professional Sewing Tips*
> *How to Sew for Children*
> *Pattern Adjustments*
> *Tailoring Suits and Coats*
> *Sewing Casual Clothes*

CONTENTS

Make your own Sportswear

...sewing ideas for teen-agers

Sportswear and separates, tailored or dressy, include those wonderfully combinable skirts, blouses, shirts, slacks, and shorts, so necessary for contemporary active living.

Although these clothes must be sturdy, they're easy to sew. They make an especially good starting point for a beginning sewer.

Making a blouse seems an easy project. Next, you need a skirt to wear with the blouse. Before you know it, an entire dress doesn't seem too complicated to make. It just takes a little time and experimentation.

The smart styling, bold colors, and easy-care qualities of sportswear are special favorites of teen-age sewers. With today's patterns, it's easy for a young miss to put her fashion imagination to work and sew up a versatile wardrobe of fashionable separates—with individual details all her own.

It's fun to make separates. The fabrics are firm and easy to work on, and are available in a range of wonderful colors. This book shows you how to use the short, simple techniques of the professional dressmaker in making smart sportswear.

Blouses

Blouses are so easy to make that you can soon sew a collection of them to mix and match with skirts.

You can sew most of your blouse with regular seams, assembling it in the same way that you would handle the top of a dress.

There are many attractive types of necklines that you can use on blouses and sportswear to lend variety to your wardrobe. You'll find instructions for making several popular styles on the following pages.

Chinese collar

The best-fitting collar of this type is cut to shape to the neck. It can be as high or low as you like. Use a pattern to cut an upper and under collar. Cut a third collar from a nonwoven, iron-down interfacing. Cut off the seam allowances on the interfacing and press to the under collar.

Sew the upper and under collars together around the edge of the interfacing to insure a uniform shape to the collar. Trim one seam to ¼ inch; trim the other one slightly narrower.

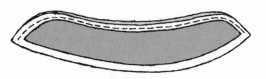

Turn to the right side and baste all around the edge.

Pin the collar to the neckline of the blouse, right side of collar to right side of neck, so that the collar meets in the center. Stitch. Pin the facing to the neckline so the collar is between blouse and facing. Stitch, then clip in on the seam around the neck and trim seam narrower. Turn

the facing to the inside and baste. Press lightly. Then remove the basting and give the collar a firm pressing. Tack facing into place on the inside of the blouse.

This collar is made and applied in the same manner on garments with either a side or center closure.

Straight collar

Make this collar on the straight of the fabric to fit the neck size. Cut a piece the length of the finished collar and twice the width, plus the seam allowances.

Press collar in half on the length.

Cut a strip of nonwoven iron-down interfacing to the finished size of the collar. Press in place along the crease line on the under side of the band. Fold the right sides of the collar together and stitch across the ends.

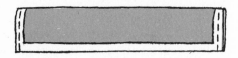

Trim the seams, turn to the right side, and press. Sew both edges of the neckband to the neckline, right sides together. Finish with the facing, as for the Chinese collar.

Tie collar

Any neckline can be made with a tie collar, which is easy to make. For a narrow tie collar with a short bow, cut a strip of fabric about 20 inches long and about 3½ inches wide. If you want a more impressive bow, measure the length and width, cut it to allow for a larger size.

If the blouse opens down the front, turn the facing to the right side and stitch the neck edge to the point where the blouse will lap.

Then clip the neck seam where the stitching line ends.

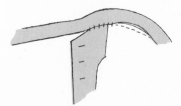

Trim the seam and turn the facing

to the inside. With right sides together, pin and stitch the tie collar to the neck, as far as the clip marks.

Be sure to start the center back of the tie at the center back neck. Fold the ends, right sides together, and stitch along the edges and across the

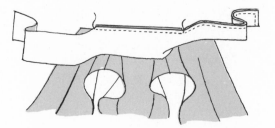

ends. Trim the seam allowance and turn to the right side. Now turn under the loose edge on the inside of the tie and slip-stitch it securely to the blouse neck to finish.

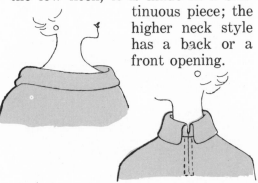

Turtle-neck collar

This collar is cut on the true bias. On the low neck, it is made in a continuous piece; the higher neck style has a back or a front opening.

Join the bias on the straight grain. Fold in half on the length and baste the edges together. Then pin the collar to the neck of the blouse and try it on. The collar should roll and stand away from the neck slightly. If it rolls too flat, the collar may have to be made smaller to fit correctly.

Some fabrics stretch more when cut on the bias than others, so it is important to test the collar before you make it. The bias can be eased in, but too much ease will spoil the collar. Adjust and sew the collar to the desired size.

Fold in half on the length and press lightly on the fold edge.

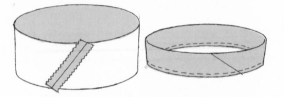

Do not make a sharp crease. Pin and stitch the right side of the collar to the right side of the neck. Trim and clip the neck seam. Press the

seam into the collar and then turn under loose edge of the collar and pin over the seam. Hold the collar taut

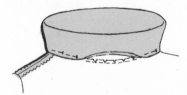

in your hands, stretching it slightly to see whether it twists.

Next, re-pin any point where the fabric of the collar begins to look slightly twisted.

The bias will stretch unevenly, so that the collar can be spoiled if this is not checked. When the collar is

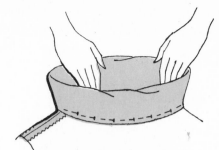

smooth, slip-stitch the inside seam.

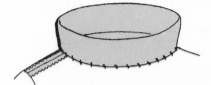

Tab neck opening

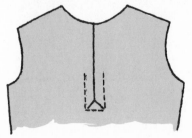

This neck, or versions of it, is used on many types of clothes, from sport shirts to pajamas. Many blouses also use this same type of opening. It is a trim, tailored neck closing, when it is properly made.

On the front, reinforce the end of the neck opening by stitching on the seam allowance line on either side and across the end. Slash into the corners. Cut four neck bands from pattern piece. Trim off the ends of three pieces, 1½ inches above the point, or on the pattern mark. Two of the bands will be used as facings. Sew these two to the sides of the front opening on the inside of the shirt, seams to the right side. The end will extend below the slash. Trim and press the seam toward the facing.

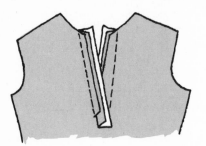

Pin and stitch the outer band to the facings, right sides together, at the neck edge.

The left end of band has point on man's sport shirt, right end of band has it on a woman's blouse. Trim the seam.

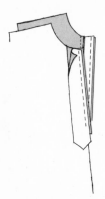

Turn the band to the outside. Then turn under the seam allowance on the loose edge and around the point.

On the underlapping band, top-stitch the band to the front. Stitch the end of this band to the shirt front between the slash marks, with the

seam turned to the right side. Now

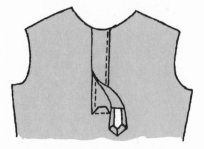

lap the upper band over the under band with the centers even. Top-stitch around the top band, and then continue around the point, and across the band above the point.

Blouse neck opening

Reinforce at the front by stitching around the lower end, as you do for a tab neck open-ing. Clip into the corners. The front bands are usually cut, facing and band in one. Fold on the length and press smoothly.

With right sides together, pin the

bands to the front edges and stitch.

Turn the facing to the inside. Turn the seam toward the band and press. Then turn under the seam allowance on facing, lap over seam and baste.

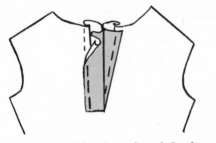

On the outside, lap the right band over the left band, matching centers. Turn to the inside. Sew the ends of the band to the front between the clipped corners.

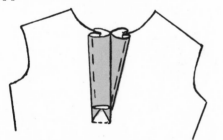

Press this seam down. Pink or overcast the raw edge. Slip-stitch the sides of bands to the blouse.

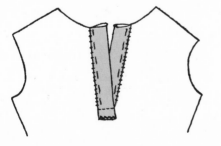

Blouse hems

If the blouse is to be worn outside, as an overblouse, it can be finished with a regular hem or facing. When the blouse tucks in, you must consider the weight of the fabric before you decide on the hem.

If the fabric is soft and fine, you can sew a seam binding to the bottom edge, turn it under, and slip-stitch it to the blouse.

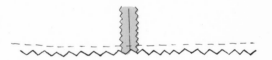

In a heavier fabric that might show a ridge under a tightly fitting skirt, sew a row of stitching $\frac{1}{4}$ inch from the lower edge of the blouse. Pink this edge. If the fabric has a

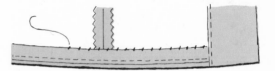

tendency to ravel, turn under the edge. Stitch two rows of stitching about $\frac{1}{4}$ inch apart.

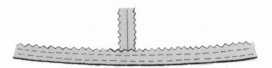

Shirred sleeve

When the full, shirred sleeve has the opening at the seam, just turn under the edge of the seam and hem it

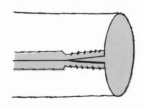

neatly to the inside of the sleeve.

If the opening is made with a slash, it must be finished with either a flat facing or bound.

Flat facing opening

If the pattern does not include a facing piece, cut one 1½ inches longer than the slash, and make it 3 inches wide at the base. Shape the facing piece to 2 inches wide at the top.

Turn and stitch outer edges of facing piece. Pin right side of facing to right side of sleeve along slash mark. Stitch from ¼ inch on either side

of the slash mark, tapering to a sharp point. Now take a stitch across the point. Then double-stitch around the point to give reinforcement.

Slash between the stitching lines to the point. Turn it to the wrong side and press. Slip-stitch the facing to inside of sleeve. Sew up underarm seam of sleeve, and press. Sew 2 rows of stitching around the lower end of the sleeve for the gathering. Then gather the

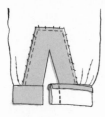

lower edge of the sleeve. Pin the right side of the wristband to the wrong side of the sleeve. Adjust the gathers to fit. Pin and stitch in place.

Fold the wristband of the sleeve with the right sides together; and then stitch the ends.

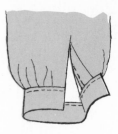

Turn to the right side. Turn under free edge of cuff band. Pin to the right side of the sleeve to cover the seam. Top-stitch.

Bound placket opening

Mark where the placket is to be sewed. Sew a stay-stitch along the placket markings. Slash to the point of the stay-stitch.

For the placket, cut a strip about 1½ inches wide, and double length of placket opening. If it's possible, you should cut along the selvage. Then fold under raw edge for ¼ inch and press. Then fold on length, so

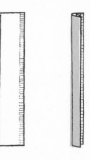

fold edge is just inside selvage edge, and press. Slide the placket piece over seam, with selvage edge on the under side. Pin in place. Now, at base of placket opening, pin so the fold edge is along the stay-stitching. Stitch on the right

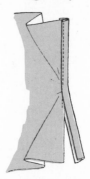

side along the fold edge of the placket piece, and the placket is finished. Finish the sleeve in same manner as

for sleeve with flat facing opening.

Skirts

Gathered skirt

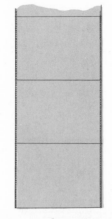

This is the easiest of all skirts to make. No fitting is necessary, and there are only straight seams to sew. Cut out the skirt pieces in lengths, unless the pattern shows it cut on the cross-grain, as for a border print skirt.

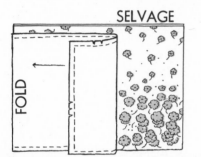

SELVAGE

FOLD

When cut in lengths, the shirring is done on the cross-grain, which gives much softer folds.

Sew up the seams, leaving part of one seam open for the placket. Then, sew the zipper into the placket (see page 19 for instructions).

As you make the gathering stitches, sew from seamline to seamline, a section at a time. This is the easiest

way to shirr in the fullness, and there is less chance of breaking the shirring thread and having to start over again. Use nylon thread in the bobbin for shirring. It is stronger and not likely to break. Sew two rows for shirring along the top edge of the skirt on the right side. The first row should be on the seam allowance line, the second nearer the skirt edge.

Make the waistband as described on page 30. Mark the band for the center back, front, and side seams. Carefully pin to the wrong side of the skirt at these same points.

Gather the fullness to fit the band.

Pin and sew the band to the skirt. Press seam toward band.

Turn under the raw edge of the band and lap it over the seamline. Then edge-stitch the band to the skirt. Now you can turn the hem of

your skirt, and give it a final pressing.

If you made any adjustments at the waistline of your basic muslin (see Creative Sewing book on *Pattern Adjustments*), they must also be made in this skirt, even though no fitting is needed. If you had to take a dart across top of skirt under belt on the muslin to make it hang correctly, make same adjustment on skirt.

Measure down on the back skirt the

depth of the alteration dart. Trim this off the top of the skirt before shirring. The skirt will hang correctly, won't dip in the back.

Straight skirt

Buy the pattern according to your hip size. The waistline can always be adjusted during the fitting. If alterations are more complicated, you'll find detailed fitting instructions, plus other valuable sewing information, in the Creative Sewing Book on *Pattern Adjustments*.

See page 19 for instructions on applying a skirt zipper, and page 30 for making the waistband.

Reversible skirt

This skirt is popular for casual wear. To make it, cut two complete skirts from the same pattern, but in contrasting fabrics. Sew up and press all the seams. Leave the placket open on each skirt. Hang the skirts for 24 hours to allow them to stretch. Pin at the waistlines, right sides together, and try on for length. Mark the length and pin the lower edges together while you have the skirt on.

Remove skirt and stitch the lower edges on the marked line. Trim off the excess fabric. Turn the skirt right

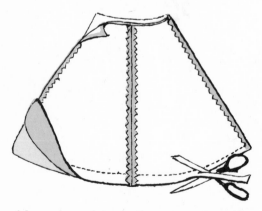

side out, and tack the seams togeth-

er, sewing with a long, loose stitch.

Finish the placket and sew on the waistband. Put in the zipper by hand.

A reversible, wrap-around skirt has one side left open. Make up skirts in contrasting fabrics. With right sides together, sew all around, leaving only waistline open. Turn skirts to right side, baste all around, and press. Sew

the waistlines together; apply the waistband. The reversible skirt can also be made by using contrasting binding to join the skirt edges.

Some fabrics are specially woven to be reversible. Sew these with a hand-finished flat fell seam, as shown on page 24.

This skirt must be bound around the edges, including the waistline. Waistband can be made in 2 lengths so that it matches both sides of the reversible skirt.

Pleated skirt

The professional dressmaker has her skirts pleated by a pleater. This is a good idea if you can have it done conveniently, since the professional pleating is permanent, more accurate.

Usually, for a regular side pleat,

you allow three times the hip measurement. If you are planning a more elaborate skirt, check with the pleater for the amount of fabric needed.

A skirt must be specially prepared before it is sent to a pleater. Decide how wide a piece of material you will need, and cut enough lengths to give the correct amount.

Fabric is never pleated with the pleats running across the grain. The fabric would be too wiry, and the pleats would not stay in place.

Sew the lengths together along the selvage so that you have one long strip. Press and turn the hem. Sew on the seam binding, and slip-stitch. The hem must also be put in before pleating. Now your fabric is prepared and ready for the pleater.

There are two ways to make this

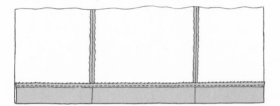

type of skirt. You can ease it onto the waistband, and allow it to hang soft from the waist. Or, you can fit the skirt to the hip, and stitch the pleats to fit the hipline.

When it hangs from the waist, the skirt should have an easy look over the hip, so allow as much as can be eased in. Sew two rows of shirring around the waistline. Use a nylon bobbin thread so the shirring won't break. Ease in the waistline on the shirring thread as much as possible. Pin the waistband to the top. Put

the skirt on and pin around the waist to check the fullness and hang of it.

If it hangs correctly over the hip,

the waist ease is right, and you can press to smooth it out. As you press, keep the pleats even at the hip, but press the fullness as it fans toward the waist of the skirt.

Sew up the side so the front pleat

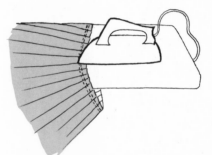

just laps over the back, forming another pleat. Sew it up to 7 inches from the top to form the placket opening of your skirt.

You will only need to sew a few snaps here. Apply the waistband. Rip the hem on back and front at the side

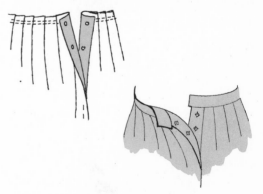

seam. Sew the seam and press it open at the hem. Next, turn up the small section of the skirt hem, and

then restitch hem back into place.

Press the pleat at this point to get a sharp line, and the skirt is finished.

If the skirt requires a back adjustment under the belt, trim off the excess material at the back of the pleated skirt before you ease the waistline. If you do not make this adjustment, your finished skirt will dip in the back, the pleats will hang open and give the entire garment an unattractive, "homemade" look.

Fitted pleats

Before you fit the skirt, baste the pleats in position at the hipline point, or about 9 inches down. Make up the

waistband and pin it around the waist. Lap the top of the skirt over the band at several points and pin right side out around the figure.

Starting at the front of the skirt, pin the edge of the pleat to the skirt and toward the waistline. Do it all around the figure, fitting as you work. More fitting will be needed at the back and hips than in the front. The pleat is tapered in at the top to shape into the skirt waistline.

Here is a professional trick. Don't just move the fold line of the pleat to the left. If you do this, the pleats will pull toward the left all around

the skirt. Instead, refold on the pleat edge, and then lap a little to the left, so that the amount you are taking in is the same on the pleat and on the lap. Then, after carefully marking the fitting line, unpin the waistband and the side seam. Remove the skirt. Measure and mark the depth pleats

are to be stitched. While the skirt is open and spread flat, edge-stitch each pleat. Be sure to follow the fitting line. Sew from the bottom of the pleat

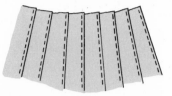

to the waistline, so that the pleat will not pucker at the end. When you have

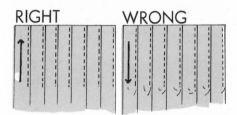

done the stitching on the skirt, finish as you do for the pleated skirt. At the side opening, stitch the pleat up to the opening, then stitch only on the pleat edge. If your skirts have a

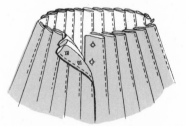

tendency to dip in the back, lift and fit this amount out of the back waistline before applying the waistband. Pleats will hang straight and sharp.

Self-pleating

On plaids, it is advisable to pleat the fabric yourself, working out the depth and size of the pleat according to the plaid. Lay the fabric on an ironing board. Fold the pleat on the plaid line. Stretch it slightly on the

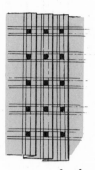

board, and carefully pin at either end of the pleat in the padding of the board to hold in place. Press with a steam iron. Pleat a section at a time until the complete skirt is pleated.

On plain fabric, you can mark the pleats from the pattern with tailor's chalk. Clip in at the pleat line at either end of the skirt.

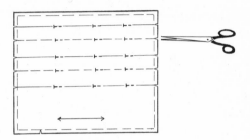

Place the fabric on the board and pin and stretch it as for a plaid. Match the clip marks at either end and the chalk marks on the length.

Press the pleats as described. After the skirt is pleated, it can be treated as you do for the commercially pleated skirt, easing or fitting it in the same way. Put in the hem as the last step on this type of skirt.

Types of pleating

There are three types of flat pleats: side, box, and inverted pleats. All other pleatings are a combination of these three basic types.

The side pleat is always folded right to left. This is the pleating professionals will use unless you choose another type pleat. When you want to pleat a skirt your-

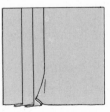

self, be sure that the side pleats are carefully laid in from right to left.

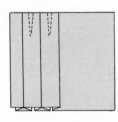

You can fit a box-pleated skirt in another way, although it is time-consuming. Take a small dart in the center of each of the pleats to fit the skirt waistline size correctly.

On fabrics that do not hold a pleat well, or that may have to be washed often, edge-stitch the pleats. After hemming the skirt, stitch from hem toward the top of your skirt along pleat edge. Inside

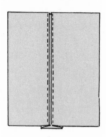

fold of the pleat can also be stitched in the same manner. It is only necessary to do one stitching.

Accordion and sunburst pleating must be done by a professional. Check with him on how to prepare fabric.

Pleats in fitted skirts

A straight skirt often has a slit or pleat to give walking room. Many types of pleats and methods of sewing them are used. The pattern usually includes instructions for the pleat. Remember that if the pleat on a straight skirt is to hang correctly, it must always be attached to the inside of the skirt.

The vent pleat and the inverted pleat are most commonly used. Both can be cut with the pleat running the entire length of the skirt, either on a fold or with a center seam.

To make the vent pleat, sew up the darts and center seam. Stitch along the pleat marking to the top of the skirt. Press the pleat to the left side, and trim away the upper section of the pleat, leaving only a seam allowance. Clip into the corner at the top of pleat and press seam open. Stitch top extension of the pleat to top of skirt. This will keep the pleat from sagging and make it hang straight.

Pleats are sometimes cut into the

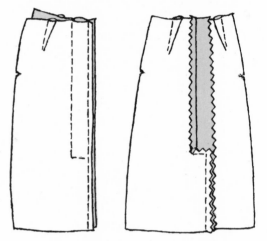

seam; these pleats often sag unless sewed correctly. Sew up the center seam, from pleat mark to top of skirt. Sew the pleat. Press it to the left side, clip the seam at the top of the pleat, and press seam open. Stitch across the top of the pleat to hold it in place. This line of stitching will show on the outside of the skirt.

The inverted pleat is made in the same way, except that an underlay

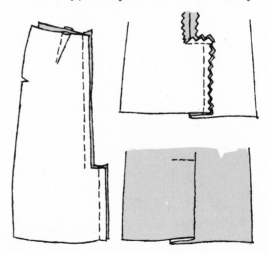

is added to form the pleat. Stitch the pleat seam from pleat mark to top of skirt. Press seam open and press pleat extensions to either side. Place right side of underlay to the pleat extensions and stitch on either side. Press and pin top of pleats to skirt. Stitch on the outside of the skirt across the top of the pleat, catching all thicknesses in place.

When the inverted type of pleat is made to run the entire length of the

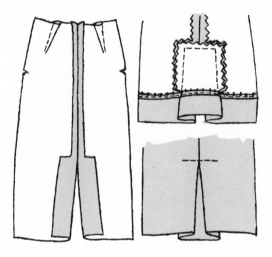

skirt, it is usually cut on a fold of the goods. Stitch on the pleat line. Then press so that it forms a box pleat on the inside. After you have pressed the pleat, stitch all thicknesses to the top of the skirt.

Skirt placket

The same type of zipper application is used for a skirt, slacks, and shorts —whether the garment opens at the side or back. Called a lapped zipper application, it makes a neater finish, and is more concealing than the slot-seam type of application.

Placket seam on the garment should be as long as the metal part of the zipper, plus $5/8$ inch seam allowance, and an extra $1/4$ inch for clearance of the zipper head. Sew up the plack-et opening, using a machine-basting stitch. Press open the seams. If the seam allowance is less than $5/8$ inch, extend it by stitch-ing seam binding along edge. Use the zipper attach-ment, adjusted to the right-hand side, for stitching. Turn the skirt inside out. Place it on the machine, with front skirt up, right sides of the front and back skirts together, back seam allowance extending.

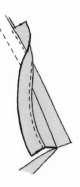

Open the zipper and place it face down on the seam allowance, teeth edge at the seam allowance line. Sew through the tape of the zipper and the back seam allowance along the

guideline indicated on zipper tape.

Close the zipper and turn right side up. The back seam allowance turns under, making a narrow fold along the zipper. Adjust the foot to the left side and sew along this fold from bottom to top of tape.

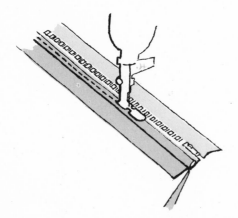

Turn garment right side out, and lightly press seam. The zipper falls under the front skirt. Stitch from side seam along bottom of the zipper, then up the side of the zipper to the top of the garment. Remove the basting thread from the placket and zipper is completed. Stitching from the bottom up prevents a puff at the

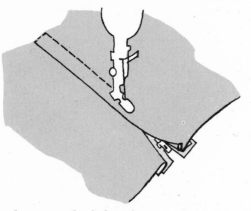

lower end of the zipper, often caused by the fabric stretching.

On dressier clothes, it is best to put in a zipper by hand. Use the same method, except sew the zipper in by hand with a small back-stitch.

Shifts

The shift is the ideal garment for a teen-age girl or any other beginning seamstress to make. It requires little fitting, and can be made up in a number of ways. By modifying the shift, and by using it in conjunction with other styles, you can easily create an impressive clothes collection. See the wardrobe planning ideas on page 50.

You can use the same pattern for jumpers, weskits, overblouses, dresses, and then pick from a variety of fabrics. All pattern companies have either shift patterns or basic-dress patterns that can be used for making the shift.

Follow your pattern in cutting and sewing the dress. If it is a sleeveless style, leave the shoulders open before facing the neckline and armhole. If your shift has a lining, sew up lining just as you do a dress, leaving shoulders open. Pin lining to neckline and armhole of dress, wrong side of lining against wrong side of dress. Sew up facings, leaving shoulder seams open.

Facing the shift

Cut facing pieces from self-fabric, and handle the facings as though the shift were not lined. This is because soft or contrasting linings have a tendency to roll out and show at the neck edges of the shift.

Now put the right side of facing against right side of the dress, and stitch to 2 inches from the end of the shoulder seam on both the neck-

line and armhole. Trim away half of the seam allowance where the neckline and armholes have been faced, and clip the seam all around. Then turn garment to right side and press.

Here's a professional trick. Turn the back shoulder'strap inside out. Slide the front shoulder strap into the back strap. The right side of

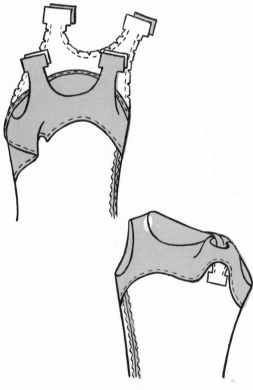

the front will be against the right side of the back. Pin front and back shoulder seams together, and sew.

The front and back facings will come together, too. Pin them and sew.

Now pull front strap even farther into back strap, so openings at sides of shoulder straps are clear. Press open the shoulder seams on the shift. Then stitch openings on either side, and trim the seam. Now pull the front

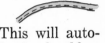

strap into position. This will automatically turn the back shoulders right side out. The whole top of the dress will be faced, with only minor tacking to be done to finish it.

You can face the unlined dress in the same manner.

When the shift has sleeves, the neckline is finished according to the style. Many patterns give several types of necklines in one pattern, or you can style your own. See the section on "Blouses," on page 7, for many necklines and collars that you can make yourself without a pattern. This is only one of the easy sewing methods that give your clothes a personalized, custom look.

Casing on a shift

If you want to make your shift with a drawstring belt, the casing is easy to make. If the dress is lined, put it on and mark at the point you want the casing. It can fall under the bust, at the natural waistline, or at a higher or lower point. Mark the line with pins. Remove the dress and put it over an ironing board, right side out. Measure and pin all around the shift, holding lining and dress together. Make sure the lining is smooth and even. Baste together all around. Stitch a line of stitching around, holding lining and dress together. Decide on the width of the casing, and sew another row of stitching at this point, parallel to the first. Make a slit in the lining seam and draw ribbon or a length of elastic through the casing. Sew it by hand on the inside of the halter.

If the belt is to tie on the outside, make worked buttonholes on the dress side of the casing, where ties will come through to the right side.

On an unlined shift, mark the position of the casing in the same way,

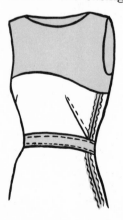

but make the casing by sewing a strip of strong, firm material on the wrong side of the dress. It can be a strip of taffeta, ribbon, bias binding, or sheath lining. Make the drawstring of elastic or fabric, as for the lined shift.

Halters

Here are two popular types of halters you can make, plus instructions for lining each of them. Any other halter will be a variation of these types; one favorite you might like to make is the drawstring style.

Drawstring halter

Pin the lining to the halter, right sides together, and stitch all around. Leave a small section of the underarm seam of the lining open. As you stitch across the neck and down the sides, leave $\frac{1}{2}$

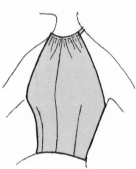

inch open at the side seam, close to the neck opening of the halter.

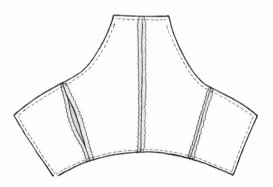

Turn the halter right side out through the opening in the lining. Baste around the edges and press.

Measure down from the neck and stitch the two thicknesses together to form the casing. Make a soft tubing $\frac{1}{2}$ inch thick, and about 20 inches long. Draw tubing through casing to form ties. (See Creative Sewing Book on *Professional Sewing Tips* for making tubing.) Make buttonholes by machine at waist. Sew on buttons.

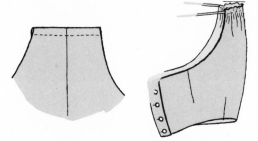

Closed-back halter

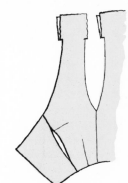

open. Turn to the right side through the lining opening. Baste and press all around. Take one back strap and push it into the end of the other strap. Pull both straps out through the lining.

The seam allowances of the straps will be together. Pin and stitch the lining ends together and halter ends together. Press seams open. Pull the straps farther out so the side seam stitching shows. Then pin and stitch the sides of the straps.

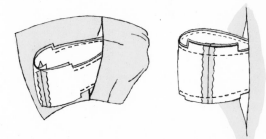

The back of the neck is joined and is sometimes pleated to give a soft drape to this style. Cut lining and halter from the same pattern. Sew them up separately. Pin the right side of the lining to the right side of the halter. Leave a small opening at the underarm seam of the lining. Stitch all around the two pieces, except at the back neck seam.

Leave 2 inches open on each strap. Trim and clip the seam all around, except where the ends have been left

Pull straps back to the right side, and the back neck is finished. Press.

If the back halter is pleated, sew the pleat after it is finished.

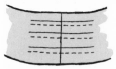

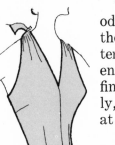

The same method is used to make the tie-back halter, except for the ends. These are finished separately, are not joined at the back neck.

Machine buttonholes are best for play clothes and bathing suits, since they are fast and easy to make. If you prefer bound buttonholes, make them before halter is lined.

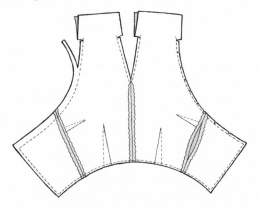

Seams

There are only four types of seams you'll need for making sportswear.

Flat-fell seam

This seam is used on shirts, blouses, pajamas, shorts, and other tailored garments. Sew a plain seam. At the side seam, press the seam toward the back. After pressing, trim the under seam allowance. Then turn under and pin or baste the upper seam edge over the trimmed seam edge. Top-stitch close to this upper seam edge, so the two rows of stitching look even. Press, and the seam is finished. Press the armhole seam toward the neck.

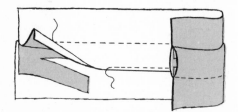

Hand-stitched fell seam

This seam is used on bulky fabrics where both sides of the seam must be finished, but the fabric is too thick to top-stitch. This seam is always made on the wrong side of the fabric.

Sew the right sides of the fabric together in a plain seam. Press to one side. Trim away the under seam. Turn under the raw edge of the upper seam and hem it in place by hand. Use it on bulky reversible fabrics.

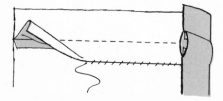

Edge- or top-stitching

Make a plain seam. Press both edges of the seam to one side. Stitch through all thicknesses of fabric on the right side along the seamline.

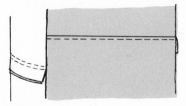

Double-top-stitched seam

This seam is often used for a decorative effect on play clothes. Stitch the seam and press it open. Then, on the outside, stitch on both sides of the seam, close to the seamline. Press to finish this decorative seam.

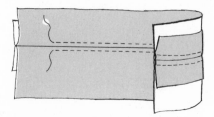

Bar tack

The bar tack is used at the end of a pocket, or to reinforce the end of the fly on slacks. Take a few vertical stitches to form a padding. Do a satin-stitch as you work over the padding and through the fabric. A bar tack can be made on a zigzag sewing machine or attachment, using a close satin-stitch to sew it.

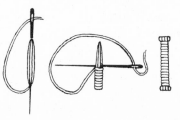

Hip pockets

This pocket is often used on skirts, slacks, and shorts. A version of it is also used on men's slacks. The ranch pocket is made on the same principle, although it is shaped a bit differently.

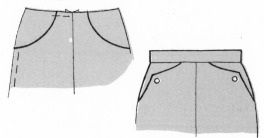

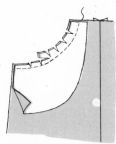

First, pin right side of the pocket facing to the right side of your garment front and stitch. Trim the seam and clip the curve. Turn pocket facing to the inside of the garment. Baste and press the edge. Pin the right side of the pocket to the right side of the facing and stitch all

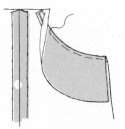

around the pocket. Stitch top edge of the pocket to the garment. Join the side seam of garment, and your hip pocket is neatly finished.

Women's slacks

Slacks have become an important part of the modern girl's casual wardrobe. They can be made of many fabrics, from denim for daytime wear to velvet or satin for evening.

Slacks can be fashionable and attractive, if they are properly fitted. The fitting is similar to that for a skirt. Hip and waist sizes are the same for slacks as on a skirt, so adjustments at these points would be the same for both. Special care is required in the fitting at the crotch and tapering of the legs. Here are some pointers that will help you give slacks a slim, custom-made look.

How to measure for slacks

Buy your slacks pattern according to hip measurement. It's important for slacks to fit as closely to size as possible at the hip, because of the shaping of the crotch. The closer to size they are at the hip, the fewer adjustments will be needed at this vital fitting point on women's slacks.

A baggy seat can ruin the trim, tailored look of your slacks.

Measure length of slacks from the side of the waistline down to the desired length. To measure for depth of crotch, sit on a straight chair and

measure from the side waistline down to the seat of the chair.

How to adjust for the crotch measurement

On the front pattern piece, draw a line from the deepest point of the front crotch across to the side seam. The length from the waist to this line should be the same as the measurement from the waist to the seat of the chair, plus ½ inch. If the crotch is too long, fold a tuck across the pattern to shorten between waist and crotch. If too short, lengthen by slashing the pattern at the same point and spreading.

If the leg needs to be shortened or lengthened, make the adjustment in the leg below the crotch.

proportion on this figure, so adjusting the darts also reduces the back waistline size. If the waistline is already correct, an extra amount can be added at side seams of slacks to compensate for deeper darts.

Check how your own waist size compares with the one shown on the printed pattern.

If the size is the same, allow a little more on the waistline as you cut, in case you need to make this back alteration on your slacks.

If the pattern measurement of the slacks is larger than your waist size, cut the slacks the same size as the paper pattern size, which will allow sufficient material to take larger darts in the back waist.

If necessary, the front waist size can be made smaller by fitting a dart from the waistline toward the hip at the side of the paper pattern.

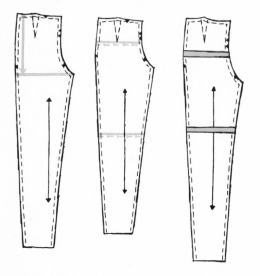

How to fit the full derriere

The front of the slacks will fit this figure fairly well, but the full back will need extra fitting. The seat needs more cupping than the pattern allows, to fit the very round hips. Take the back darts in deeper to give the slacks more cupping, smoother fit.

Usually, the waistline is smaller in

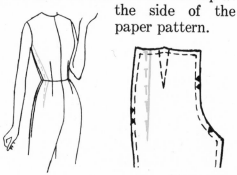

If the slacks are already cut, make

the waistline smaller by fitting out the extra fullness at the side seam. Be sure to make the same adjustment in future patterns.

The very round derriere requires additional fitting. This figure is usually narrow across the hips, with all the fullness in the back. Back of the slacks needs a greater curve and more width at the back crotch seam. Add this amount at the back inseam of the slacks.

How to fit the flat derriere

With this type of figure, the seat of the slacks will droop and be too large. First, adjust as you do for the same problem on a skirt. Take a fold across back under waistline, tapering it to nothing on either side.

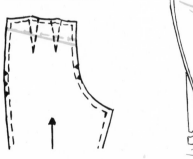

If the seat still looks too full, the darts are giving more cupping than is needed for the flat derriere. Rip out the darts and make each one a little more shallow.

Fit out the extra fullness at the side. Take a deeper seam from waistline to hipline, tapering the seam to nothing below the hip.

Make the adjustment in the pattern by taking in the same amount with a fold from waist to hip, tapering to nothing, on one side of pattern.

If the slacks are too round below the fullest part of the hip, make the back crotch smaller by pinning a tuck just back of the crotch seam on the back only. This eliminates the extra fullness. Pin this same tuck in the pattern. Rip out and recut crotch seam from the adjusted pattern.

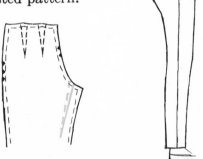

If you use a pattern from another pattern company, it may be necessary to refit the crotch. Slope of the back crotch seam may vary with the pattern-maker. The degree of slope is the only point you will need to check. Basic adjustments will be the same.

Pattern companies now make proportioned slacks which fit for height, but the depth of the crotch is an individual problem not necessarily dependent on height. Even the proportioned slacks pattern may require some additional adjustments.

Cutting slacks

Adjust the pattern carefully to your correct size before you cut. Check the type of fabric you are using to see if it has a nap or other surface that indicates it must be cut with all pieces running one direction.

Check the grain line to be sure it is straight as you lay out the pattern. Measure from the grain line to the selvage as you pin the pattern in place. This is important to the correct hang of the slacks.

Cut the waistband on the length or cross-grain. It will be interlined to prevent stretching. Lay out all the pieces before cutting. Cut, following the adjusted pattern; no additional allowances are needed.

Sewing slacks

Mark darts, pocket placement, and other detail before removing the pattern. Some patterns indicate a mark for the crease line. Put pins along this line to mark it, as you do for darts. Remove the pattern, and sew the darts in the front and back pieces.

Before sewing the seams, it's important to press the crease in the front and back of the leg. Place the front of the slacks on an ironing board, right side down. Fold one side back along the crease mark so the right side of half the leg is facing up. Press carefully along this line.

Usually, this crease runs into the waistline dart which becomes a continuation of the crease. Back sections of the slacks are pressed in the same way, except that the crease is made 8 inches from the waistline, regardless of the back fitting darts.

If no crease line is given on the pattern, fold the leg, wrong sides together, with the inside and outside seam edges even. Now, press along

the fold and this will give the correct crease line on the leg.

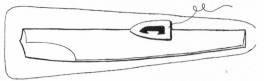

Join the back and front pieces at the side seams. A side pocket can be put in as you sew the seams, just as for the ranch-type pocket, page 25.

Next, join the inside leg seams. This is the method used for making men's slacks. This

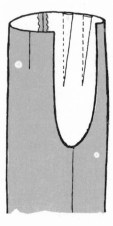

type of assembly makes the slacks hang more smoothly.

If the slacks have a side seam zipper closure, sew the zipper in on the left side, as shown on page 19.

Many women prefer the zipper down the back, which gives a smoother fit at the sides and doesn't interfere with the side pocket. If you want a back zipper, sew up the center front and continue it toward the back.

Leave the back seam open for a 7- or 9-inch zipper, whichever is best.

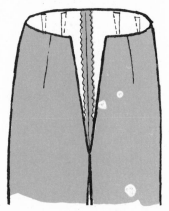

Apply the back zipper with a lapped seam type of application, just as for a side placket type closure.

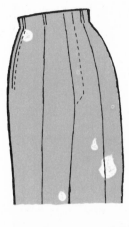

Or, if you prefer the fly-front type of slacks, for a slimmer, and generally more flattering appearance, it is not difficult to convert a pattern to this type. The placket, or the fly, starts at about 2 inches up from the crotch seam. Stitch about 2 inches toward the front. Clip the seam at this point. Only this much seam is sewed at the back so that it is easier to insert the zipper. If you like, you can sew all the back seam, just leaving the front open from the 2-inch mark. Use a special trouser zipper for the fly-front to give a neat closure.

Your pattern will show two right fly facings and one left fly facing. If the fabric is lightweight, these can be cut from the same fabric. If your slacks are of a heavy fabric, face the right fly pieces with a lining fabric. Put the right sides of the two right fly pieces together, stitch them all around. Leave just the top edge open. Turn right side out and press.

Turn back and stitch ¼ inch on the outside edge of the left fly facing. Then sew the left facing to the left front opening of the slacks, after placing the right sides together.

Clip and trim the seam and press the seam to the inside.

Place the zipper right side down at the right front opening, with the

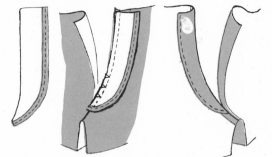

tape of the zipper along the seam edge. Sew as close as possible to the teeth of the zipper with the zipper foot on your sewing machine.

Turn the zipper right side up. The seam allowance is turned back. Slide your right facing piece under the zipper with about ½ inch extending beyond the zipper tape. (It will depend on the width of the right fly piece. It should extend under the zipper for the width of the seam allowance.)

Stitch along the fold edge of the seam, close to the zipper. Catch fly piece in stitching, as you sew.

Now, lap the left front to seam allowance line, and then pin or baste in place.

Turn the slacks to the wrong side. The tape of the zipper will now be

against the left facing only. Pin the tape just to the facing. Sew the tape close to the zipper teeth, using the zipper foot. Then sew a second row of stitching on the edge of the zipper tape and turn the slacks to the right side. Fold the right fly extension back. Then mark and stitch on the outside of the slacks; be sure to catch back the left facing. Extension will now fall in place under the zipper. Reinforce the lower end of

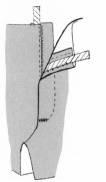

the fly on the right side with a bar tack, catching all thicknesses of material with the tack. If the zipper is longer than the placket, unzip it and cut it off at the top when the waistband is sewed on to the slacks.

The next step is to sew up the back crotch seam. Nylon thread is the best choice for this seam on women's slacks. It is strong, and has needed elasticity which will stretch with your body as you bend or sit.

Men's slacks can also be sewed with nylon thread for added strength and elasticity. (See section on men's slacks for another sewing method.)

Making the waistband

There are three methods for putting the waistband on women's slacks and skirts. All three can be done by machine; the choice of method depends on the fabric that you are using.

Lightweight fabric

Press the waistband in half on the length. Cut a strip of medium-weight, nonwoven interfacing the width of half the band, less the seam allow-

ances at either end. Lay the interfacing along the fold line on one side of the band. Stitch it into position all around.

Fold right sides of the waistband together and stitch across the ends.

Then turn right side out and press. Turn back the seam allowances on the length of the belt and press.

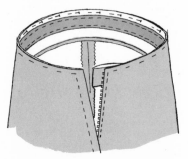

Pin the interfacing side of the band to the inside of the slacks. The front edge of the band should be lined up even with the edge of the placket opening. On the fly front, the edge will be even with left side of the front opening. Stitch the waistband to the slacks, along the crease line.

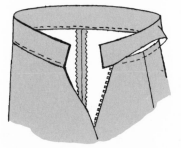

Press the waistline seam into the waistband and turn under the seam allowance on the loose edge of the waist-

band. Pin to the right side of the

slacks and stitch. It isn't necessary to trim the seam at the waistline.

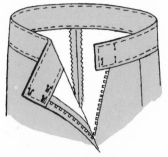

Medium-weight fabric

Cut the waistband on the length of the fabric along the selvage. If no selvage edge is available, bind one edge of the fabric with seam binding.

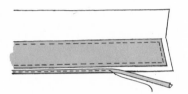

Press in half on the length. Cut an interfacing of nonwoven fabric, the width of the band, minus seam allowances. Stitch to the inside of the band on the selvage or bound side. (Nonwoven interfacings with an adherent are also available. These can be pressed on, eliminating the need for sewing interfacing into waistband.)

Sew the ends, turn to right side and press ends. Turn back seam allowance on the length of the band and press. Pin the right side of the waistband to the right side of the slacks (the unlined side) and stitch. Drop

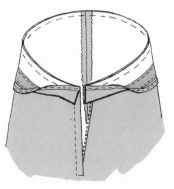

the selvage or the bound side of the belt to the inside. Pin into place on right side and stitch.

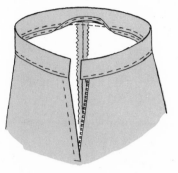

No seam allowance is turned back on the inside band. It lies flat against the slacks which makes the waistline look and feel less bulky.

Heavyweight fabric

Cut the belt on the lengthwise or crosswise of the fabric. Fold in half on the length and press. Trim off one side of the band ½ inch from the fold. Buy grosgrain ribbon or belting, half the width of the waistband. Use this ribbon or belting as a facing. Sew it to the cut-away side of the band along the fold line.

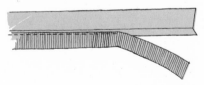

Sew the ends of the belt. Then sew

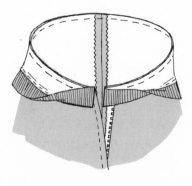

together the right side of the waistband and the right side of the slacks.

Stitch along the seamline on the right side to hold band in position.

These same methods can also be

used on skirts and women's slacks. Choose the one most suitable for the weight of your fabric.

If the trouser zipper is too long for the front opening of the slacks, zip the head down and cut off the extra length of zipper at the waistline of the slacks.

Sew the waistband to the slacks, catching the tape of the zipper in the waistline seam. This acts as the stop for the top of the zipper. The zipper head locks into place at any point when the tab is depressed.

On men's slacks, waistband is made in two pieces, a left and a right side band. See instructions for making the fly-front closure, on page 29. Method is same for men's, women's.

Men's slacks

Patterns for men's slacks do not come in proportioned sizes. Instead, the pattern gives a waist and inseam size. Buy the slack pattern according to the correct size of the waist.

Measure a man for the inseam and outside seam for the correct length. Compare inseam measurement to the one given on the pattern. If the pattern has to be made longer or shorter, check outside seam measure of the pattern before you make the alteration. On the front slack pattern piece, measure from waistline to the finished length on the outside seamline. If it must be lengthened or shortened the same amount as for the inseam, then make necessary adjustment across leg below crotch. Pattern indicates where you should make this alteration.

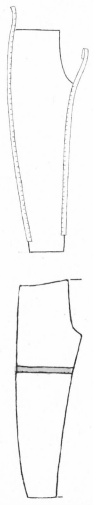

If the outside seam measures longer or shorter in proportion to the inseam measurement, make an adjustment between waist and crotch.

For example, the inseam measurement is 32 inches, and the outseam measures $43\frac{1}{2}$ inches; when you compare these to the pattern, you find the inseam of the pattern is 32 inches, but outseam measures only 42½ inches. Add extra 1 inch of length to the length of the crotch (right).

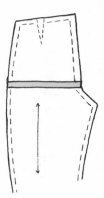

Follow the pattern guide as you lay out the pattern for cutting. Before cutting the back, add extra fabric on the center back for a let-out seam. Add by tapering from nothing at the seat to 1½ inches at back waistline. Add the same amount to the waistband length.

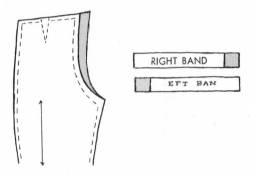

RIGHT BAND

EFT BAN

Mark the fabric carefully for darts, pockets, and other detail. Also, be sure to mark original back seam.

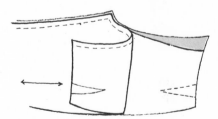

Sew in the back darts first. Press carefully. Put in the back pockets next. In lightweight fabric, the back pockets can be made of the same fabric as the slacks. In heavier fabric, make the pockets from a lining fabric, but face with self-fabric.

Each pattern company has its own shaped pocket piece. Some show the

pocket made from two pieces; others show the pocket in one. The principle in making them is the same. Cut the facing strips 2½ inches wide for the pockets. Then sew strips to pocket on the pattern piece markings (A).

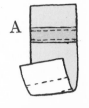

A

Mark the correct position of the back pocket on the slacks with basting stitches (B).

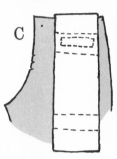

B

Pin the pocket piece to right side of slacks, matching marks, but sew around the basting mark from wrong side, forming rectangle (C).

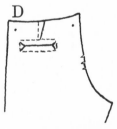

C

Slash the fabric through center of stitching to ½ inch of either corner. Then clip to corners (D).

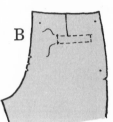

D

Turn the pocket piece to the inside of your garment through the slash. Fold lower pocket to form a welt. Stitch welt by machine on the right side (E). Sew ends of pocket on the inside, as for a buttonhole. Trim off the top of this pocket piece one inch above the pocket slash (F).

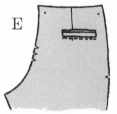

E

Fold the pocket, with outsides together, along the fold line. (For two-

F

piece pocket, pin the two pieces with the outsides together.) Stitch the two pocket pieces together close to the edge (G).

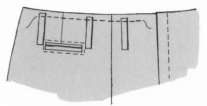

Turn the pocket right side out and stitch again, turning under edges of upper pocket (H).

From the outside, turn slacks down from waist, and stitch across the top of pocket seam (I).

Press it from the right side, then top-stitch the upper seam through all thicknesses of the pocket (J).

Next, stitch the top of pocket to waistline of slacks.

Before joining the side seams, press the crease line in on both back and front slacks, as you do for women's slacks. Follow the same procedure for joining the seam, sewing the side pockets, and finishing the fly.

The back seam on men's slacks is finished differently. Put the waistband on first, before you sew the back. Belt carriers must be made before the waistband is sewed. Cut a strip of fabric long enough for eight belt carriers, 1½ inches wide. Turn the edges in ¼ inch. Press. Fold in half and edge-stitch each side.

Cut the fabric strip into lengths

and sew one edge of each strip to the waistline of trousers where marked.

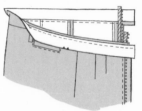

Unzip the zipper and sew the right and left waistband to the right side of the slacks. After sewing in place,

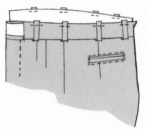

cut off the ends of the extended zipper. Sew the belt carriers to the top of the slacks' waistband before you sew the facing.

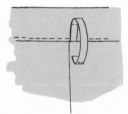

If you prefer the belt lower on the waistband, sew the belt carriers lower. Press them so they extend over the waistband for about ¾ inch. Turn under the edge ¼ inch and sew the belt carriers to the trousers about ¾ inch below seamline of the man's slacks' waistband.

The left front waistband will extend beyond the edge of the slacks. Turn the waistband to the outside.

Cut the waistband lining on the

bias. Press back on the fold line and cut a strip of nonwoven interfacing the width of the finished facing piece. Stitch this strip to the inside of the facing, just under the seamline and inside the fold edge.

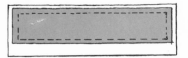

Stitch the end of the left waistband to the facing, with the right sides together, and then press the seam toward the facing.

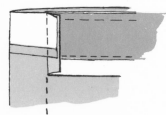

Stitch the upper edge of the waistband and facing together around the waistline. Then trim the seam close.

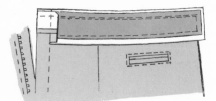

Turn the facing and left front waistband to the inside and press. Baste through the seam from the right side, catching the facing.

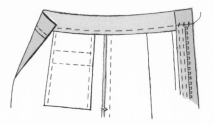

Stitch on the waistband side close to the edge of the fabric.

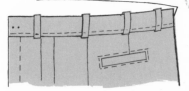

Pin and stitch the right side of the facing to the right side of the waistband. Sew across the front end that extends beyond the fly.

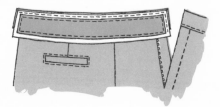

Trim the seam, turn the facing to the inside and press. Baste from the right side, holding facing in place. Edge-stitch along waistband seam.

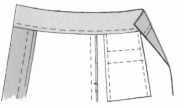

On the lightweight fabrics, the back seam can be sewed with nylon thread, as shown on women's slacks. Sew to the middle of the waistband on the original stitching line.

Press the back seam open, turn under the seam edges and tack the let-out seam to the inside facing.

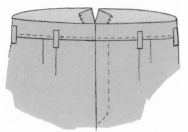

In heavier fabric, sew the back for about 3 inches from the crotch seam.

Leave the seat open for about 9 inches. Sew up the upper back and waistband, as for lighter fabrics.

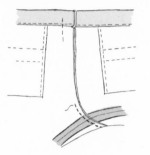

Sew up the back seat by hand, using buttonhole twist and a back-stitch

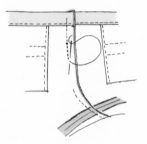

for a sturdy seam. This will give elasticity to the seat. Make a buttonhole on the left side of the waistband and on the pocket in the back.

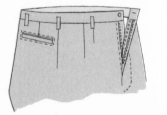

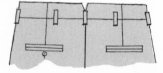

Sewing notions departments sell a large hook that can be used at the waistline of men's slacks instead of the usual buttonhole and button.

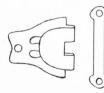

Making cuffs

on slacks

Turn the bottom of the slacks to the right side at the length he desires. Finished length of the slacks varies with fashion and the man's taste.

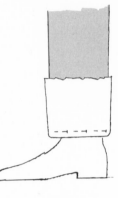

Measure and baste the length all around. Measure up 1½ inches from this line and fold down.

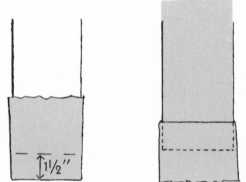

This line is the edge of the cuff. Press this fold. Turn under the remaining length to the inside and catch-stitch to the inside of the leg.

Press again, and the cuff is finished. Turn down the cuff at the side and inseam and loosely tack the seams together about ½ inch from the top edge of the slack cuff. You can also use this method in altering the length of all men's slacks.

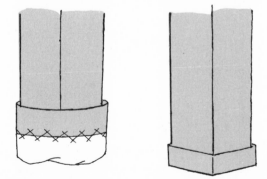

Sport shirts

Men's and women's sport shirts are made exactly alike, with one exception. A man's shirt buttons left over right, a woman's buttons right over left. Both shirts can be sewed completely by machine, and require little fitting. There are many styles of sport shirts, but this is the basic method for making them all.

Men's measurements

Buy a man's shirt pattern according to chest measurement. Although the neck size is also shown on the pattern, it makes little difference in cutting, since the sport shirt collar does not fit tightly, as a dress shirt does.

If the man's neck is much larger than the pattern size, increase neck size by cutting the neckline slightly larger and increasing collar size.

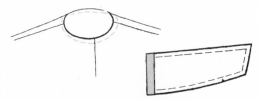

In rare cases, the shoulder width may need to be adjusted. If the pattern shoulder is too wide, it can be made narrower by a fold through the yoke and into the front shoulder.

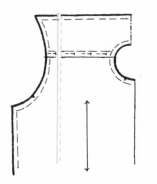

The back of the shirt can be made smaller simply by shirring in or pleating the excess, according to the back style of the sport shirt.

Length of sleeve is important in all types of shirts. If the sleeve is too long, it is in the way; and if it is too short, it binds uncomfortably as the cuff slides up the arm.

Measure the man's sleeve from the center back of the neck to the wrist for sleeve length. If the shoulders need to be narrowed, make this adjustment before you measure for the length of the pattern sleeve.

The pattern for a man's shirt shows chest measurement and sleeve length for size. For example, a pattern with a size 38-inch chest will have a 33-inch sleeve length. If the shirt you plan to make requires a 35-inch sleeve, you should cut through the sleeve and add the two extra inches in 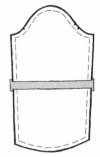 length. If you narrowed the shoulder ½ inch, you will need to lengthen the shirt sleeve 2½ inches.

Also check the length of the shirt before it is cut. Measure from the

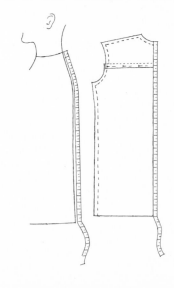

back of the neck to the shirt length he prefers. Pin the yoke to the back of the shirt pattern and measure this length. If it must be made longer, add length to the shirt bottom, unless there is detail, such as side vents. In that case, cut across the shirt between the waist and hip and lengthen the shirt at that point.

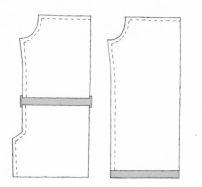

Women's measurements

The shoulder width on a woman's shirt can be altered in a similar manner to a dress. If the shoulder needs to be narrowed ½ inch in a dress, then narrow it the same amount in a shirt. If the waistline needs lengthening or shortening in a dress pattern, then adjust it in the shirt pattern for the same amount.

Lengthen or shorten the sleeve the amount adjusted on a regular pattern sleeve. Always take a woman's arm length from the top of the shoulder to the wrist, so the shoulder adjustment will not affect the sleeve length.

Sometimes, a woman's shirt will have a small bust dart to give some shaping over the bust, but a shirt does not follow the contour of the figure, as a dress does.

If the bust is extremely full and required a deeper dart fitted on the basic muslin, it's a good idea to fit a similar dart in the shirt.

The front of the shirt will have to be made longer to allow for the dart,

but this extra fitting will make the sport shirt more becoming and comfortable for a woman with a full figure.

As you can see, both men's and women's sport shirts require only a minimum of fitting.

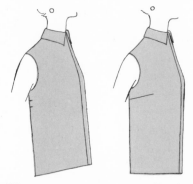

Wrong   Right

Cutting the shirt

Be sure to follow the grain lines of the pattern in cutting a shirt. If the shirt is plaid, match the plaid at back and front armholes. Yokes, collars, and cuffs are always cut on the length grain, except when the fabric

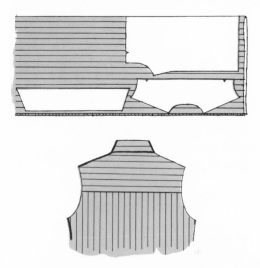

has a pattern or nap that makes it one-directional. Then it is cut with all pieces one way. A shirt yoke is always cut with a facing. On lightweight fabric, cut the yoke of self-fabric. If the sport shirt is in a wool material, line the yoke with a thin silk, rayon twill, or soft taffeta fabric for a more professionally-made look.

Sewing the shirt

Make pockets, cuffs, and collar first. Interface the collar and cuffs, using any fine, crisp cotton, such as lawn or cambric, a fine linen, organdy, or a commercial woven interfacing to give them added body.

Sew your interfacing to the inside of the under collar at the seam allowance line. Put the right side of the under collar to the right side of the upper collar and then stitch the two all around the edge.

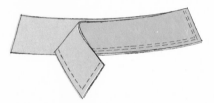

If nonwoven interfacing is used, cut off the seam allowance around the outside edge before sewing it to the collar. Never catch the interfacing seam allowance in with the seam. This also applies to the cuff.

Trim the seams slightly less than

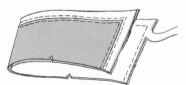

$\frac{1}{4}$ inch. Turn to the right side and

baste, then press all around. Make the cuff in the same way. If the collar is to have a trimming stitch, do it after the collar has been pressed.

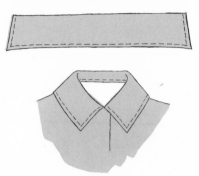

Sew the trimming stitch on the cuff after the cuff has been sewed to the shirt sleeve.

Make the shirt pocket as shown in your pattern instruction sheet.

Mark the shirt for placement of the pocket, the center front line, and the fold line of the facing on the front shirt piece. Remove the pattern. Then you can press the facing back on the fold line.

Turn under $\frac{1}{4}$ inch seam allowance at the outside edge of the facing and then stitch.

Pin the pocket in place and stitch it to the shirt. It can be edge-stitched or sewed in about $\frac{1}{4}$ inch, whichever method you prefer.

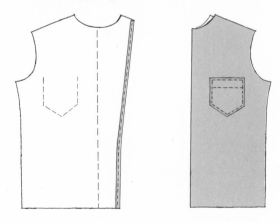

Put a clip mark at the top of the center back shirt. Mark for the back shirt fullness. If fullness is unpressed pleats, clip at the pleat marks. If it is shirred, clip at the marks for the shirring. Mark all the notches on all pieces as you go. Then remove the pattern from the fabric.

If the shirt back has pleats, fold them into place, and stitch them at the seam allowance line.

Sew the shirring in with a large stitch on the machine. Sew one row of stitching from one shirring mark to another on the seam allowance line. Then do a second line of stitching $\frac{1}{4}$ inch from the edge.

Mark the notches on the yoke pieces. Mark the center back at the neck and lower edge. Then remove the pattern from the pieces.

Pin the right side of the yoke facing to the inside of the shirt, matching the center clip marks and the side notches. If it has shirring, ease into place by shirring it on the bobbin thread on the machine.

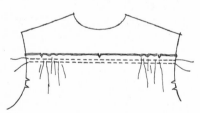

Pin the rest of the yoke to the back shirt on the shirring line. Sew on this line. Pin the right side of the yoke to the right side of the shirt on the original stitching line. Stitch along this line. If the yoke is striped or plaid, be sure you do the stitching along a straight line of the stripe.

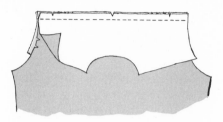

Press this seam carefully. If the yoke is to be edge-stitched, you can do it at this point. Sew it on the right side.

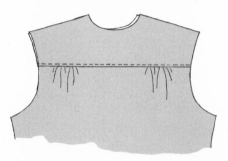

Pin and sew the right side of the yoke facing to the wrong side of the shirt front. Then press the seam toward the shirt yoke.

Turn under the seam allowance on the yoke and pin it to the shirt front, so that it just laps the original stitch-

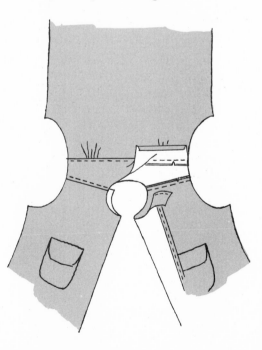

ing line that you have sewed. Next, edge-stitch it along the fold edge. The front yoke can also be sewed to the shirt with an inside seam. Now, turn under the front edge of the yoke and pin it to the front shoulder seam, so the seam is between the yokes. Pin for the entire length of the seam on the inside. As you do, the yoke at the shoulder will be turned inside out for that short length. Sew it this way. Pull the yoke back in place and

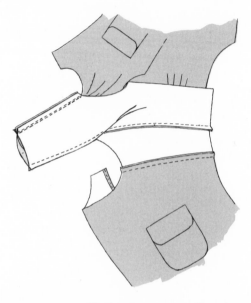

the seam will be between the two yoke pieces. This is the preferred method for sewing it. Press the seam and then you're ready to do the edge-stitching on the shirt yoke.

At this point, sew on the collar. It is easy to apply while the shirt is open. Since this is a convertible collar, you will need to make a loop for the neck closing.

Make a handmade loop of thread. Or, use a self-fabric one, best for convenience and quality. Cut a short piece of bias 1 inch wide and 1 inch longer than the finished loop. Fold the bias lengthwise, with the right sides together, and stitch about ¼ inch from the fold.

Stretch the bias as you sew. Trim

the seam ⅛ inch. Turn the bias and form loop by sewing ends together.

Tailored collar

Mark the center back of the collar with a clip mark. Match the back of the under collar to the center back of the neck and pin around the back, from shoulder seam to shoulder seam. Pin the front of the collar from the center front line of the shirt to the shoulder line; but in the front, pin the upper and under collars together. Now sew the loop to the shirt neck.

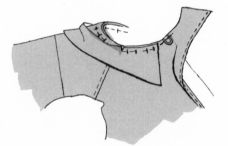

Slash to the seam allowance line, on the upper collar where it is loose at the shoulder seam.

Fold the front facing back over the front neck so that the collar edges are between the facing and neck. Then turn under a seam allowance at the top of the facing.

Stitch around the neck, catching the facing, double collar, and neck in the front. As you stitch, fold the upper collar back at the shoulder line so just the under collar is stitched to the back neck. Continue around, catching the facings and the front collar edges to the front neck of the shirt as you sew.

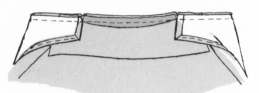

Trim the seam at the front neck. Clip into the seam allowance at intervals around the neck curve, to keep the neck from drawing.

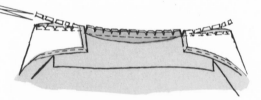

At the shoulder seam, clip the neck and the under collar to the stitching.

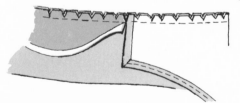

Turn the facings to the inside. Turn the back neck seam into the collar. Fold under the loose edge of the up-

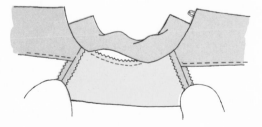

per collar and pin it over the neck seam to cover the raw neck edge.

The top edge of the neck facing and the edge of the back collar can be machine-stitched in place.

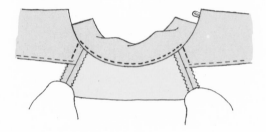

Sleeve placket

From the pattern, mark the sleeve for the placket. Then stitch the point at the end where it is to be slashed. The placket is made up of

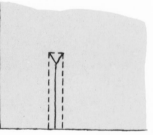

the underlap and overlap. Cut the underlap from the pattern piece so that one edge is on the selvage. Fold over ¼ inch on the other edge and press. Fold again, so the first fold edge comes just inside the selvage edge, and press.

Slide the folded piece over the back edge of the slash. The selvage edge will then be to the wrong side of the sleeve. Next, pin and stitch along the fold edge. The underlap is sewed in place in one stitching.

Turn under the seam allowance on overlap, as shown below right. Then

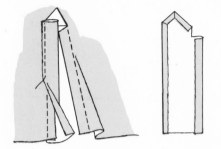

baste or press. Lap the edges together and press on the length.

The next step is to stitch the right side of the overlap to the wrong side of the front slash edge and press the seam toward the overlap.

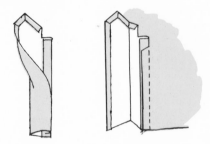

Fold the overlap to position along the seamline and pin. Then pin the overlap to the sleeve, with the point in the center. Pin across the overlap, catching the underlap at the end of of the placket opening.

Then stitch the overlap, starting across the band, to hold the underlap secure, around the point, and down the side, to complete the placket.

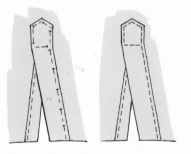

Assembling the shirt

The sleeves can now be sewed in the shirt. Pin the right side of the sleeve to the right side of the armhole and stitch. Trim the shirt seam to about ¼ inch. Press the sleeve seam toward the shirt. Turn under ¼ inch of the sleeve seam and baste or pin to the shirt. Stitch along the edge an even distance from the original stitching line. If you can stitch it

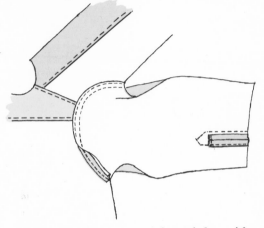

more evenly from the right side, the seam should be basted rather than pinned. Now, press this seam, which is called a flat-fell seam.

With the right sides together, pin and stitch the underarm seam and

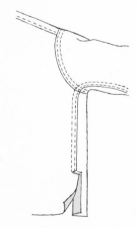

sleeve for the entire length. Trim the back seam allowance to ¼ inch. Press the seam toward the back of the shirt. Turn under the edge of the front seam and pin or baste to the back. Stitch the entire seam allowance as you do for the armhole seam. It's easier to stitch this seam on the shirt from the inside.

Regular cuff

You are now ready to attach the cuff. Gather or pleat the lower edge of the shirt sleeve, whichever the pattern shows. Pin the right side of the under cuff to the wrong side of your shirt sleeve and stitch.

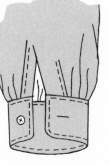

Turn under the loose edge of the upper cuff and pin to the right side of the sleeve, just to cover stitching. Next, edge-stitch this across the top of your shirt cuff.

Now stitch the cuff all around, as you do on the edge of the collar. The stitching should be made the same width from the edge of cuff.

French cuff

On the French cuff, the underlap of the placket is turned under the wrong side of the sleeve. It does not extend into the cuff. The right side of the cuff is sewed to the inside of the shirt sleeve at the first stitching, because this type of cuff folds back on itself, and the under cuff becomes the outer cuff after it's finished.

Roll-up sleeve

This is a straight shirt sleeve, made with no cuff so that it can be rolled up. On a sport shirt, the underarm seam is a flat-fell seam, which is finished on either side, so that the sleeve need only be hemmed.

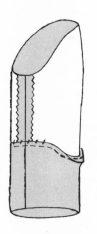

When this sleeve is used on a woman's blouse, you do not use a flat-fell seam. Here is one method you may use.

Cut your sleeve long enough to make a deep hem, around 8 inches. Fold under sleeve edge and stitch. Turn the deep hem to the inside and slip-stitch. The sleeve can be rolled up with a clean seam at the cuff.

Hemming a shirt

The sport shirt is finished either with a straight hem all around, or with side vents. The pattern usually shows both these finishes.

Turn the lower edge of the shirt under ¼ inch and press. Fold the right side of the facing to the right side of the front shirt. Stitch the facing and front together along the hemline. Turn the facing under and press. Fold back the hem at the hemline, stitch, and press.

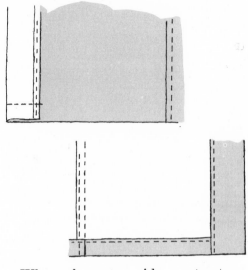

When there are side vents, turn under the outside edge and press. Fold the right side of the vent to the right side of the shirt, as you do for the facing, and stitch along hemline. Turn vent to inside, pin, and stitch.

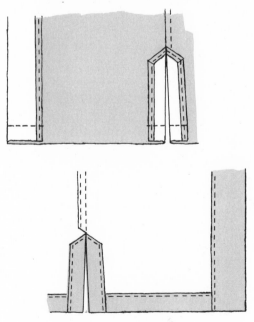

If possible, make machine buttonholes. A woman's shirt is made the same way, except that the buttonholes go on the right instead of the left.

Bathing suits

It's easy to make a dressmaker bathing suit. The method is similar to that used for making shorts or a halter, except that the bathing suit is

lined. A bathing suit pattern always includes an inside lining pattern piece that looks like short bloomers. You can use this piece in any of your favorite shorts patterns to convert them to bathing suits.

Make up the shorts by the pattern, but leave the back seam open for a zipper. Do not sew on the waistband. Cut the lining pants of cotton jersey or fine wool jersey, if you want quicker drying. (Some of the synthetic blends also offer quick-drying properties.) Cut an additional strip of lining about 6 inches wide from the center back and front pattern for shadow panels. They also finish the inside seam so there is no chafing. Sew up the crotch seam of the pants, and the same seam on the panels. Then press open the seams.

Put wrong side of panel to wrong side of lining; turn under raw edges of panel, pin and stitch to the lining.

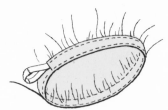

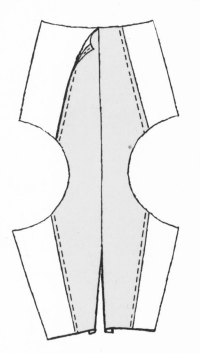

Pin and stitch the waistline of the lining pants to the waistline of the shorts. Turn under the raw edges of the placket opening and pin to the tape of the zipper of the shorts. Finish by hand.

Sew the waistband to the shorts; lining pants are sewed in at the

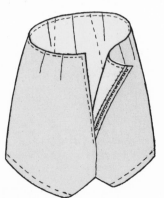

Sew up the rest of lining, leaving the back seam open for the placket. Turn a hem at the leg of the lining pants, or sew a bias binding. Then stitch the binding, or hem to form a

casing. Stitch around the edge of the leg so that the elastic will stay flat and not curl or roll up.

Cut an elastic band, 1 inch smaller than the thigh and draw it through the casing. Join elastic by hand.

same time. As you sew, be sure wrong side of lining is against the wrong side of the pants. The shorts can also be attached to a top to make a one-piece type of bathing suit.

Bikini or bloomer suit

The lining for this suit is cut from the same pattern as the bikini itself. Sew up the suit and lining. Turn lining and shorts so that seam allowances are to the outside. Pin and sew the lining to the legs of the shorts. (See illustration.) Trim and

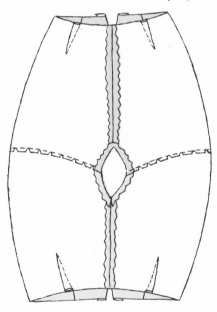

clip leg seams. Turn so the lining is

inside shorts, with wrong sides together. Baste and press leg seams. Sew row of stitching about ½ inch from edge of leg to form casing.

Rip the inside crotch seam on the lining at the casing. Then draw the elastic through the casing and join the ends by hand.

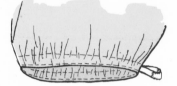

If the top of the bloomers has a waistband, finish it as you do for the dressmaker bathing suit. If top has no band, finish with an inside seam by stitching to lining. Sew an inside seam through placket opening.

Sew a tape in the waist to prevent stretching. Finish the lining to the tape of the zipper, as you do for the dressmaker bathing suit. Sew a hook at the waist to finish.

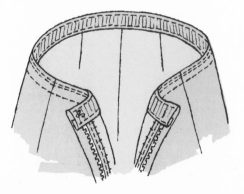

Strapless bra top

Lining can be of jersey or a firm, thin cotton. Cut lining and bra from the same pattern. Sew them up separately. Sew feather boning to the lining at the outside of the bustline and at the side back under the shoulder blades. Cut boning to fit just inside the seam allowance. Leave an open-

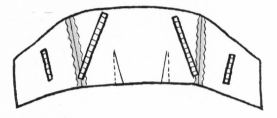

ing at the underarm seam of the lining. Pin and sew the right sides together, trim, and clip the seam allowance. Turn to the right side through the lining opening. Press all around. Shoulder straps can be made to hook on, if you desire.

This type of bathing suit top can

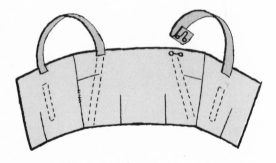

be made flat across the front, or you can use a tie-front style for a softer look, if you prefer.

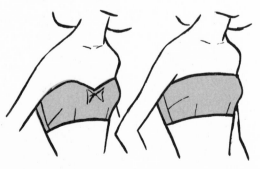

Men's trunks

Matching beach shirts and men's bathing trunks in bright colors and patterns have become quite popular, and they are easy to make.

First, cut the trunks from the pattern, and then cut a lining from the same pattern. Use a cotton jersey for the lining fabric. Sew up all the seams of the trunks with flat-fell seams. Use a regular seam on the lining. Sew a double panel in the lining shorts, as the pattern shows.

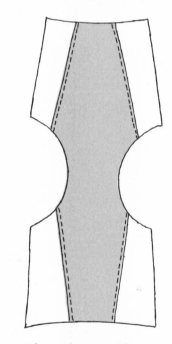

Turn the edge of the trunk leg back $\frac{1}{4}$ inch and press. Turn and pin one inch, and hem by machine.

Sew a $\frac{1}{2}$-inch hem at each leg on the lining shorts to form a casing.

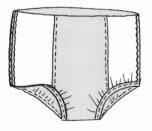

Draw elastic, cut one inch shorter than the thigh measurement, through the casing. Sew the ends by hand.

Cut a wide elastic 1½ inches smaller than the waist measurement. Divide and mark the elastic into four equal parts. Join the ends. Lap the elastic ½ inch over the edge of the trunks, placing one of the markings at the center front, sides, and back.

Pin at these points. Stitch close to the edge, stretching the elastic to fit.

Turn the elastic to the inside. Baste the lining so it comes under the edge of the elastic.

Stitch the lower edge of the elastic, stretching it to fit the inside, catching lining in same stitching.

Make several more rows of stitching between, stretching the elastic as you sew it in place.

Make sure the elastic is strong, so that it snaps back to size after sewing. Too-soft elastic will stretch and make the waist size too large.

See the section on sport shirts, page 37, for instructions on how to make a man's beach shirt to match the bathing trunks.

View A

Wardrobe planning with the shift

To make this costume, cut shift to length you want. When cutting fronts, add seam allowance, and make two pieces. Add patch pockets and zipper it up the front. Use shift pattern with sleeve; a Chinese collar can be added later. Make slacks to match or contrast.

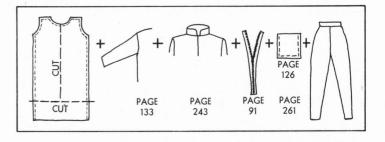

CUT

CUT

PAGE 133 + PAGE 243 + PAGE 91 + PAGE 126 + PAGE 261

The shift can be cut below the waist or below the hip for wear over shorts or slacks. Make it up in both versions as colorful additions to your wardrobe. You might make the short top in a solid color, with sleeves and collar in a contrasting shade. Try a bold pattern for the tunic style. For either style, add a bias collar and sleeves. Make up slacks or shorts to match or contrast with the top.

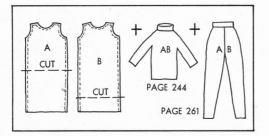

A
CUT

B
CUT

+ AB + A B

PAGE 244

PAGE 261

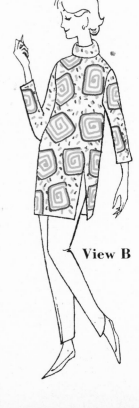

View A

View B

Here's the same basic pattern made up in a full-length shift, or cut off for a fashionable overblouse. Both versions are flattering for sports or casual daytime wear. Add a shirt-type sleeve and a neat tab neckline with a Peter Pan collar. Make them both up in jersey or a double-knit fabric to add another dimension to your flexible sportswear wardrobe.

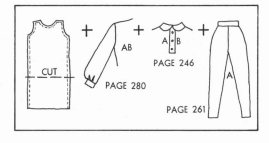

View B

View A

The versatile shift can be made in dressy styles for afternoon or evening wear, just as easily as it can be made into sportswear. Choose dress-up fabrics. Add a tie-belt and sleeves for an afternoon dress. Or, cut a V-neck, eliminate the sleeves, and add to the length for an elegant evening look. The tie-belt can be added at the waist, up under the bust, or even at the hipline for variety.

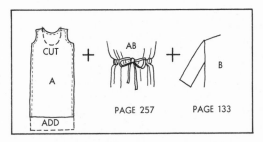

View A **View B**

In the style shown at far left, the basic shift is cut to hip length. Measure from back neck to hip, or length desired. Cut neckline to a V. Measure from base of throat for depth. Allow for hem at hip and seam allowance at neck. View at left is cut to the desired length. Armholes and neckline are bound; use self-binding or a commercial one. Add a slim skirt and tie-belt for a smart 2-piece dress.

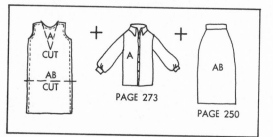

Here are two attractive variations of the shift for beachwear or sports. The shift is again cut short and, in one version, is slit at either side to make a beach dress. Cut the same style shorter for wear over shorts. Try a variation in neckline, too. Remember that the mixing of colors and interesting prints will make your wardrobe more varied.

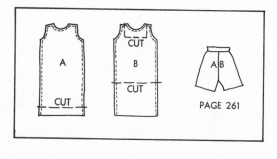

View A **View B**

Sewing leather sportswear

Leather garments have been made and worn for centuries, but only in the last few years has the home dressmaker become aware of leather's possibilities. Home dressmaking follows ready-to-wear trends. As leather has made its appearance in more ready-to-wear fashions, home sewers have become interested in duplicating them, especially in casual clothes.

Obtaining skins was once a problem. Now you can buy leather in the piece-goods department of your local store or in the hobby shops scattered throughout the country. The hobby shops generally have a much greater variety of skins, and are also expert in helping you select the most suitable leather. They also can help you estimate the amount you need.

Selecting a pattern

As you can see from the fashion magazines, almost any type of garment that you want can be made of leather.

On page 61 is a random sampling of popular leather fashions. You will notice that most of the styles are either two-piece, or are designed so that they do not require full-length pieces of leather. Although you can get hides large enough to cut a full-length coat, most leather garments are made from small animals, and can take advantage of the smaller hides. Clothes are designed so they can be cut from the smaller hides with a minimum of piecing.

For your first attempt in sewing leather, it's wise to pick a simple garment until you become more familiar with how to work it. A hat, vest, jerkin, overblouse, or skirt can be made easily by a beginning sewer.

After you have selected a pattern, take only the pieces you need from the envelope. If the back, or any other piece, is to be cut on a fold, make a duplicate of it. Then, paste it together so you have a complete piece, rather than a half.

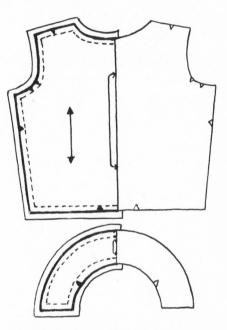

The pattern only gives one front, so make a duplicate of it also, so you will be sure to cut a pair.

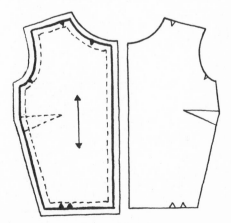

Duplicate all of the pattern pieces in this manner. The reason for this is that you never cut leather on a fold. Also this method makes it easier to estimate the number of skins that you will need for the garment.

The full hide is usually sold in the smaller skins. A full hide, or a half hide or side can be purchased in the larger skins. Take your pattern with you, and the dealer can help you select the correct amount of leather, as well as suggest the best hide for the garment. Record the amount you use for each item. This will help you later when you are figuring amounts for other garments.

Like fabric, there is a length- and cross-grain to leather. As in fabric, the length-grain is the strongest; the cross-grain will bulge and hang unevenly after it is sewed.

The length-grain on leather is the grain that runs along the backbone of the animal. If you cut your leather garment so the grain of the leather follows the up-and-down line of your body, you'll have no difficulty with the hang and fit of the garment.

Although there is a grain to leather, there is no nap. You can lay the pattern pieces going up and down, as long as they are on the length.

Be sure the garment you are making is in the right size. Leather can be taken in if made too large, and taken up if too long, but stitch marks will show if the leather is let out.

If you pin your pattern to the leather, only put pins in the seam allowance so pin marks won't show in the body of the garment. An even better method is to secure the pattern with cellophane tape. You can cut through the tape easily as you cut the pattern. Use sharp shears and cut with long, even strokes.

Machine-stitching

Always sew leather with silk thread. Use a longer stitch on your sewing machine—about 7 to 10 stitches per inch. Test your machine for tension and pressure adjustment. Leather is rather thick and spongy, therefore the presser foot should be raised enough to allow it to pass freely through the machine. Always check tensions before sewing on any new fabric to be sure the stitch is balanced, tensions properly adjusted.

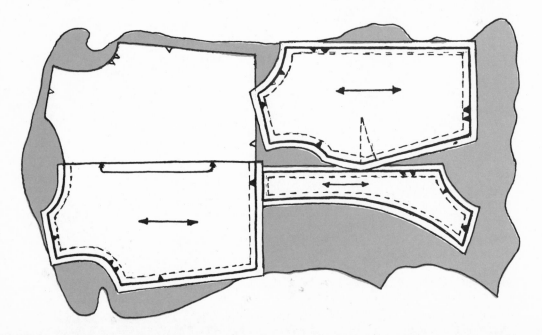

Seams on leather

Always sew seams from the top down on leather. Never back-stitch by machine; it cuts the leather. The best way to secure the seam is to tie the thread. After all seams are sewed, finish each by applying rubber cement along it. (Hobby shops have a special

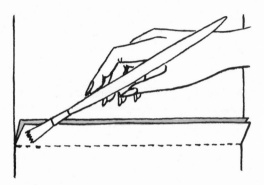

cement for leather.) Open seam, pound with mallet. Seam can then be raised and allowed to relax into place.

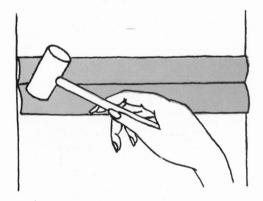

Curved seams should be notched so there will be less bulk when they

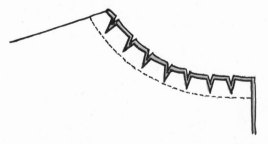

are turned. This improves garment.

Mark and sew all darts. Marking can be done on the wrong side with tailor's chalk, a colored pencil, or a ballpoint pen. Then, cut away dart, leaving about a ½-inch seam. Open as close toward the point as possible.

Finish like a seam, with rubber cement, and then pound with a mallet.

Long seams are inclined to stretch when sewing leather. To prevent this, it helps to sew seam binding into the seam. Cut the seam binding the length of the seam. Measure binding with the pattern seam. Apply cellophane tape on the binding at intervals for length of seam, and sew.

Making a leather skirt

A 4-gore skirt with a slight flare is an easy one to make. Be sure gores are cut on the length-grain of the skin. Leather skirts should always be lined. Cut the lining from the same pattern as the skirt. Taffeta, China silk, or one of the new sheath linings can be used. Sew up the seams of the skirt, leaving a placket opening for the zipper. Rubber-cement and pound back the seams, including the seams at the opening for the zipper. Sew the zipper in by hand, using silk thread and sewing it with a back-stitch.

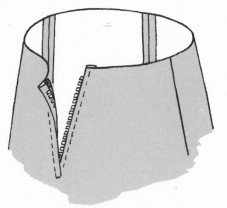

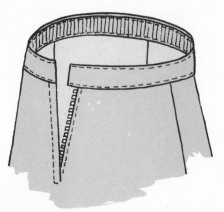

Make up the lining and sew it to waistline of the skirt, with wrong sides together. Tack lining to the zipper by hand on the inside. Cut a waistband of the leather 2½ inches wide and 3 inches longer than your waist size. Sew one edge of the waistband to the top of your skirt. The band should extend ½ inch beyond the front placket, and 2½ inches beyond the back. Turn under ½ inch at the top edge of the waistband. Ce-

on the leather side. Turn up the hem, put rubber cement along top edge of hem only for a smoother hem.

Try your hand at some of the small items made from leather. You'll gain confidence in handling it. Then you will be ready to make a coat.

Leather coats

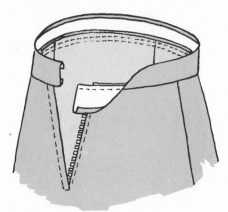

ment it and pound it in place. Cut 1-inch grosgrain ribbon the same length as the waistband. Put right sides of the ribbon and band together and stitch the short ends, taking ½-inch seams. Turn the ribbon to the inside, facing the waistband. Stitch it in place at both edges of the waistband

Select your coat pattern, and be sure you choose one that is suitable for leather. (Some patterns are now made especially for leather.) Take your pattern with you when you buy your skins. With your pattern along, you will be sure to get the right amount. The best part of making a coat in leather is that if it has to be pieced, piecing often enhances it.

Look through fashion magazines and visit shops specializing in leather fashions. This may inspire you to make something that's really high-style. In fact, it is often a good idea to choose a simple, basic coat pattern, and then design the detail and adjust the pattern before you select skins.

Full-length coats can be cut of large hides with little piecing. When you choose smaller hides and piecing is necessary, use the piecing seams to create design detail on the coat. (See illustration B below).

Here are some style ideas, and how to execute them.

Coat pattern A

Ready-to-wear coat

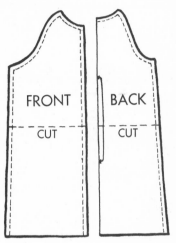

Pattern adjustments

Coat pattern B

Ready-to-wear coat

Pattern adjustments

Note: Where the pattern has been cut, it is necessary to add 1-inch seam allowances. Be sure to add them to the pattern before you cut your leather coat.

Lining leather coats and jackets

Cut and sew the linings for leather garments as you would for any wool coat or jacket. Linings can be made from any fabric you choose. Dressy coats can be lined with taffeta or satin; sport-type coats can use a plaid or fake fur. Follow the fashions, and choose a lining you prefer.

It is difficult to sew a lining to leather, so use the method furriers use. Cut a strip of bias 1½ inches wide from the lining fabric. Make a fine cording by covering cord (#24 cable cord) with the bias. Use the cording foot on your sewing machine. Sew the cord along the inside edge of the facing, with the raw edges of the cording along the edge of the fac-

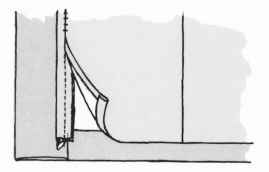

ing. On a coat, the lining and coat hems can be left free, as you do on a regular fabric coat. Use French tacks at all seams of the coat.

When lining a jacket, sew the bias

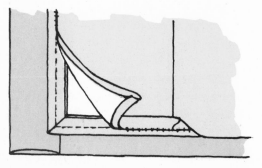

along the hem as well as the facing, so the lining can be tacked all around. Sew the linings in jacket by hand.

Special detail on leather

These are the preferred methods for finishing certain details on leather garments. These techniques work better on leather, and give your garments a professionally-made look.

Buttonholes

Make them like the cord-bound buttonhole, described in the Creative Sewing Book on *Professional Sewing Tips*. Use #9 cable cord for lips of buttonhole, as for wool. You needn't cut leather on the bias to make the cord, however. After you cover the bias, cut away one side of seam allowance, so there will be graduated thicknesses when it is finished.

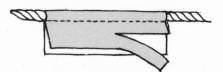

When you are sewing the cord to the tissue paper guide, cut side of bias cord should be facing down.

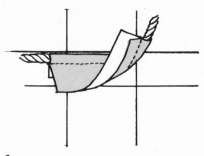

Belts

Tie belts are especially smart on leather fashions. Narrow ones can be made in soft, fine leathers. Heavier leathers are suitable for wider ones.

Leather tubing

To make tubing, cut a strip of leather just double size of the finished tubing you want to make, plus seam allowance. Fold the right side over cable cord in the size of the finished tubing, right side of the leather to the inside. Here's a trick to make the leather handle more easily. Rub a light coating of a facial cream on the right side of the leather. Stitch leather around the cord, using the cording foot on your sewing machine.

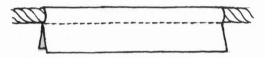

Tubing is made in the same way as buttonhole cord, except that a heavier cable cord is used. Trim the seam to $\frac{1}{8}$ inch and pull out cable cord.

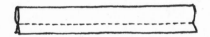

With an ordinary safety pin, turn the tubing. The light coating of facial cream will make it slide easily inside out. Wipe the leather clean with cleansing tissue. *Don't use this method on suede or suede-type leathers.*

Tubing can also be made by folding the wrong side of the leather over cording, and then stitching with the cording foot on your sewing machine. Trim seam very close to the stitching. The cord can be left in as a filler for a more firm belt, or it can be removed to make a softer tubing.

This belt is also shown in a heavier version. You can make it by sewing over a thicker cable cord. The leather should be soft, and pliable; leave cording inside to keep it tubular.

One-inch tie belting

Cut a strip of leather the desired length, and $2\frac{1}{4}$ inches wide. Turn under $\frac{1}{4}$ inch along one edge. Rubber cement it down and pound with a mallet. Turn the other edge of the belt and lap to the fold edge. Cement this edge and pound with the mallet. Cut the short ends on an angle.

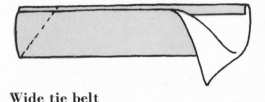

Wide tie belt

Cut a strip of leather the length you desire, and twice the width of the finished belt, plus seam allowances. Fold in half on the length, with right sides together. Sew the seam, leaving a small opening at the center for

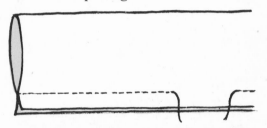

turning the belt. Fold the belt so the seam falls in the center of the back. Press seam open and cement in place. Sew across the ends of the belt. Then

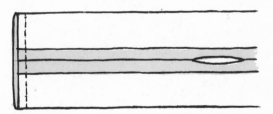

turn the belt right side out through the opening in the center back. Press with steam and a press cloth; then stitch around the edge, if desired. Sew up the back opening by hand.

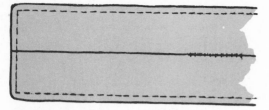

Pockets

Welt and flap pockets are two styles frequently used on leather sportswear and casual clothes. Make these pockets in the same way that you would when using a fabric.

When making a patch pocket on leather, sew on the right side and re-inforce it. If one row of stitching is used, sew around the pocket about ¼ inch in at the top, and then back to the stitching, forming a triangle.

When you sew on the outside flaps,

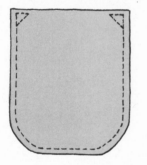

tack with extra stitching at both ends to hold them down. You can do this by hand with buttonhole twist.

When you stitch a pocket that has double stitching, start at the bottom and stitch around, across one corner, down, and around the pocket, forming the second row of stitching and then stitch across the opposite corner, down the outside edge, and around the bottom, where stitching

will meet. Always pull the thread through and tie to the inside to hold.

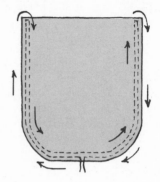

Sleeves

Sleeves in leather garments should be cut a little long. After leather is worn for awhile, wrinkles will form from the bending of the arm. These are essentially permanent, so plan the sleeve length accordingly.

Hems and finishing

Hems in leather coats and jackets can be made the same as hems in skirts.

Neck edges and armholes of jerkins and overblouses can be turned under and cemented into place, then stitched all around. On a soft thin leather, you can use self-leather to face them, with seams graded and notched to eliminate bulk. Then cement in place and pound the seams with a mallet.

Much of the detail on leather can be done as it is on wool. When you come to a sewing point on leather that you have never tried before, it's best to experiment first on scraps.

If you are hesitant about making a major piece of clothing, such as a coat, from leather, cut it in muslin first to be sure it fits correctly and is the design line that you want. (See Creative Sewing Book on *Pattern Adjustments* for information on making a muslin, and fitting instructions.)

Sport fashions from leather

Hand-stitches for leather

Hand-stitching used on leather is the same as for fabrics. The most common stitches are the running-stitch, back-stitch, and the slip-stitch, with which you are familiar. Another one that is frequently used is the glove-stitch, described below.

Glove-stitch

This stitch is made with a punching

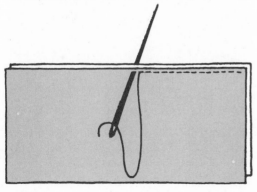

motion. Stick the needle through the leather and complete the stitch. Then bring your needle back to the other side and complete stitch. It resem-

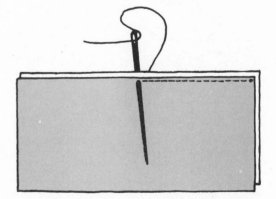

bles a small running-stitch, but only one stitch is taken at a time. It's used on the extreme edge of a seam, as on gloves. It can also be applied as an edge-stitching around lapel or collar, or used on a hand-sewed pocket.

INDEX